Pink Trees Press

In *Naming a Hurricane*, Madeline Artenberg engages in an honest, thoughtful, and, most important, artful exploration of herself and the people around her. A "disturbance" begins early on, as she recounts experiences with parents not far removed from their immigrant roots. This low-pressure system resolves into a storm and then a full-blown hurricane as rough childhood transitions into an open-hearted, sometimes tempest-tossed, adulthood. As the hurricane "dissipates," parents pass, lovers leave marks, and memories remain. In the clear light of day, a deep self-knowledge is revealed. We can learn much from it. — Thaddeus Rutkowski, author of *Tricks of Light*

Naming a Hurricane is an apt title for Madeline Artenberg's brilliantly seductive collection, a memoir in verse, that takes us into the turmoil of being a "Jew-girl" in America. Her childhood is textured by a grandfather who wrote "from right to left", a grandmother whose "breasts hung like worries", and a father's love, all powerless to shield her from ever-present storms. With terse lyricism, penetrating lucidity and sensuality, the poet's barometric shifts leave the reader breathless. *Naming a Hurricane* is not only a dive into diverse and dark subject matter, a marvelous "soup of misshapen dumplings", but celebrates a life illuminated by poetry and passion. This is a riveting and daring collection, one that will not leave your hands until you have read it from cover to cover. —Stephanie Dickinson, author of *Blue Swan Black Swan: The Trakl Diaries*

In Madeline Artenberg's poetry collection, *Naming a Hurricane*, the sections are labeled with scientific terms for the progress of a hurricane: Disturbance, Low Pressure, Storm, Hurricane, and Dissipation. These terms also metaphorically echo the human events evoking the poems. *Naming a Hurricane* has been a long time in the making. In that time, the poems have transformed both dramatically and subtly. They viscerally embody all manner of storm and calm.

> "Plain Jane" / they called her. / "I don't need any of you," / she'd say. / Today, she belongs / to a choir. Sunday morning, / her white robe / glistens. Underneath, / Jesus soothes the fresh welts, / darkly rainbowed.

In the poems, there is travel to Greece under a military junta; and there is travel from fear and rage, to acceptance. Madeline Artenberg has, indeed, named the hurricane, with language that is a match for its force. — Estha Weiner, author of *This Insubstantial Pageant*

Madeline Artenberg is first and foremost a consummate storyteller. In her new volume of poetry, *Naming a Hurricane*, she brings us rich and compelling stories drawn from her life in the diaspora of immigrant New York City. She takes us on her journey from doting granddaughter to the formidable artist she is today. Her brilliant choice to structure this collection within the narrative device of severe weather gives these poems momentum and power that drives this temporal travelogue into a dazzling chronicle of a life lived fiercely. This poet is exquisitely sensitive while simultaneously tough as nails. She creates searing emotional experiences for the reader, then brings us home safely by the final stanza. Within the joy or pain of each experience described, we always learn something new. These poems are a window into our souls, manifested by the poet's lyrical command of language and her gift for finding the rhythm and center of each experience. Much like the Gotham that created her, Madeline's poems charge ahead without apology. She writes about incredibly difficult topics with an emotional honesty that makes these subjects universally accessible: child abuse, sexual harassment, love, death, and lust. The reader comes away from this collection with an appreciation for the power of this hurricane. —Rick Christiansen, co-editor of the forthcoming *The Dead Pets Anthology*, Spring 2023

Madeline Artenberg's *Naming a Hurricane* blasts us into every moment we could never admit to another or even ourselves, and just as a hurricane grows from a far-away disturbance into a furious storm, each piece erupts hidden truths with breathtaking words. These poems cut through our hearts, offering us relief that comes from finally saying out loud: love, rage and delicious desire. Indeed, this stunning collection takes us on a ride through a hurricane and brings us to hope. —C.O. Moed, author of *It Was Her New York*

Madeline Artenberg's *Naming a Hurricane* elegantly transports you through a whirlwind of richly-worded verse. Beautiful are the recollections of Grandma and Grandpa "…plucked from Eastern Europe replanted across ocean…" and the recollections of "blueberry cheese danish" and thoughts "of the Old Country." Like the words in her poem "Holiday in Pamplona," Madeline's poetry "…stays steady on the stones slippery with blood and fear…running safely ahead of horns and hooves…" and is "alive at the end." You will feel the exhilaration as you ride the tempest with her. —Jerry T. Johnson, Author of "Poets Should Not Write About Politics", *Evening Street Press;* Winner of the *Evening Street Press* 2020 Sinclair Poetry Prize

In the years that I've known and worked with Madeline Artenberg, she has grown as both a person and a poet, as is evidenced in *Naming a Hurricane*. This is the work of a mature poet who is both courageous and wise. It is an honest and heart-felt collection that represents 30 years of Artenberg's best writing. I urge you to accompany her on this very human, often painful, but beautifully poetic journey. She names her hurricane, struggles through the storm of it and finally triumphs as she metaphorically passes through to the other side "Unfolded, /…still flush…" —Chocolate Waters, author of *Muddying the Holy Waters*

NAMING
A
HURRICANE

NAMING

A

HURRICANE

Madeline Artenberg

Poems

Pink Trees Press

Titles from Pink Trees Press

Origami Book #1, Linda Kleinbub
Origami Book #2, Linda Kleinbub
Silver Tongued Devil Anthology, Linda Kleinbub &
Anthony C. Murphy, Editors
Poems from an Unending Pandemic, Phillip Giambri
Dysfunction: A Play on Words in the Familiar, Pauline Findlay
Good Boy, Bad Boy, A Better Man, Phillip Giambri
Naming a Hurricane, Madeline Artenberg.

Copyright © 2023 by Madeline Artenberg
Published in the United States of America by Pink Trees Press
First Printing January 2023

Library of Congress Control Number: 2023900531
ISBN: 978-1-66640-025-0

Acknowledgments

Thank you to the editors who included the following poems in their publications:

7 Train Anthology: "On Stravinsky's 'Rites of Spring'"; *100K Poets for Change*: "Lot's Wife"; *AbsintheLiteraryReview.com*: "Path of Mary Magdalene" (previously published as "Gospel of Mary Magdalene"); *AbsintheLiteraryReview.com:* "Sister"; *And Then:* "Feels Quite Natural"; *And Then*: "Hitching in Dallas"; *And Then*: "Trouble"; *ANYD Anthology:* "At the Gorilla Forest"; *ANYD Anthology:* "Buzz"; *Appleseeds Anthology:* "Chosen Seats"; *BigCityLit:* "Apostle"; *BigCityLit*: "At the Butterfly Conservatory"; *BigCityLit:* "Sister"; *Brownstone Anthology:* "Buzz"; *Caprice:* "Disappearances"; *Caprice*: "Thefts"; *Caprice*: "Trouble"; *Downtown Newspaper*: "Blessed Work" (previously published as "All Angels Church"); *Ducts.org*: "Hitching in Dallas"; *erbacce:* "Apostle"; *erbacce*: "Sister"; *Green Pavilion Anthology:* "The Gardener"; *How Dirty Girls Come Clean:* "Bouquet"; *How Dirty Girls Come Clean*: "Brooklyn Rush Hour" (previously "Rush Hour to Brooklyn"); *How Dirty Girls Come Clean:* "Rock Chick Sonata"; *Leisure/Dinner with the Muse:"* At the Gorilla Forest"; *Literary Parrot vol 1:* "Supper Time"; *Literary Parrot vol 2:* "Apostle"; *Literature Today International Journal of Contemporary Writing:* "Batter"; *MacQueen's Quinterly (MacQ-11):* "Crak, Bam"; *MacQueen's Quinterly (MacQ-11):* "Offspring"; *MacQueen's Quinterly (MacQ-11)*: "Rhinestones and Memories"; *MacQueen's Quinterly (MacQ-11):* "Soft Hand"; *Maintenant 11:* "All in a Row"; *Margie, The American Journal of Poetry:* "Disappearances"; *Medicinal Purposes*: "My Eyes are Tantalized" (previously published as "Fifty-One"); *Mudfish:* "A Kid and a Dog"; *Mudfish*: "Ruse of the

Flute"; *Nomad's Choir Journal*: "Brooklyn Rush Hour" (previously "Rush Hour to Brooklyn"); *Nomad's Choir Journal*: "Buzz"; *Nomad's Choir Journal*: "Mango Mad on the Island of Grenada"; *Nomad's Choir Journal*: "On Stravinsky's 'Rites of Spring'"; *Nomad's Choir Journal*: "The Gardener"; *Nomad's Choir Journal*: "Tibet, Land of the Snows" (published as "In the Land of the Snows"); *October Babies*: "Supper Time"; *Poetrycentral.com*: "Chosen Seats"; *Poetrycentral.com*: "Tibet, Land of the Snows" (published as "In the Land of the Snows"); *Poets Wear Prada Bug Book*: "Buzz"; *Poets Wear Prada/Rainbow Project (green)*: "The Blind Man and Poet"; *Pudding House*: "Tibet, Land of the Snows" (published as "In the Land of the Snows"); *Rant*: "Brooklyn Rush Hour" (previously "Rush Hour to Brooklyn"); *Rattle*: "Guardians of the Good"; *Red Fez*: "After Death"; *Red Fez*: "Babel"; *Red Fez*: "Batter"; *Red Fez*: "My Eyes are Tantalized"; *Red Fez*: "Queen of the Late Bloomers"; *Rogue Scholars*: "A Jew in Texas"; *Rogue Scholars*: "Bouquet"; *Rogue Scholars*: "Disappearances"; *Salonika*: "Bouquet"; *Shabdagucha*: "The Gardener"; *Silver Tongued Devil Anthology*: "Guardians of the Good"; *Spinsters: Women Period*: "Path of Mary Magdalene" (previously published as "Gospel of Mary Magdalene"); *Spiny Babbler*: "From Nothing"; *Stone Poetry: Dead Pet Anthology*: "Namesake"; *THE POET: Culture & Identity*: "At Ellis Island"; *THE POET: Culture & Identity*: "Batter"; *THE POET: Culture & Identity*: 'Old Pictures"; *THE POET: War & Battle*: "Sister"; *THE POET: War & Battle*: "Tibet, Land of the Snows" (published as "In the Land of the Snows"); *Up Against the Wall Mother*: "Soft Hand"; *Vernacular*: "At the Gorilla Forest, Bronx, NY"; *Wormwood Press: Lies*: "The Apple Merchant"; *Wormwood Press: Revenge*: "Lot's Wife"

Dedicated
to
Iris N. Schwartz, Sheryl H. Simler,
Mireya Perez, Barbara Minch,
Ella Smith, and Betsy Goldsmith

From the Author

This once silent, bullied, friendless girl thanks you for going on this journey with me! I grew my voice through experience, friendship, and poems, one by one. As a kid, my saviors were Howdy Doody, Mr. Rogers, Lucy, Nancy Drew, the bookmobile, Dick Clark, Soul Train, Perry Mason, Elizabeth Taylor, James Bond, and my grandparents. I didn't realize it, but my earliest writing was nightly prayers of just desserts for my abusers. Every time I took two steps forward and then fell back, I gave up, but the open road was as enticing as a novel. I would never look at the last page of a story first, so I ventured I had to keep going on the road and learn to trust it. The biggest proof was that I transformed "why me?" into comedy skits, plays, and poetry. I grew up hiding everything. Sweetest irony is that, as a new poet, I was immediately appreciated for my family and sexually-themed poems. The floodgates of honesty were wide open! One of the joys in recent years is that "me, only" turned into "me, too!"

In public school, I couldn't speak in class, except to raise my hand first with the answer. I won the medal for best overall student in the public school 6th-grade graduating class. Only three people clapped in Assembly. Finally, I made my first friend at eleven and a half years old. I thought I was so smart. I didn't know a damn thing until I threw myself into the world after college graduation: I was wife, failed Spanish teacher, disco queen, cocktail waitress, world traveler, wife again, actress, licensed hypnotist, Media Buyer and Planner, peace activist, and photojournalist. The photo agency told me I should crawl on my belly or shimmy up a pole to get better shots. The minute my first poem shot out, I sold my cameras. I immediately understood that only I could birth my poems.

When I was a kid and the doorbell rang, my mother would push me under the kitchen table, clasp her hand over my mouth as I yelled, "We're here! Don't go!" Well, readers, I'm here now, so here we go!

Following are the dear ones who got me to this point, this book. Thank you for everything:

Iris N. Schwartz, Sheryl H. Simler, and Mireya Perez: friends since the beginning of my poetry career; Barbara Minch: friend, artist and poet; Linda Kleinbub: friend, publisher, editor, photographer and writer; Phillip Giambri: friend, editor, and writer; Pauline Findlay: friend, editor, writer, and originator of book concept of hurricane stages; C.O. Moed: friend, editor, and writer; Linda Wulkan: extraordinary book-cover artist; Betsy Goldsmith: friend from Brooklyn projects; Joyce Barrie: creator of The Humor Playshop; Denise Duhamel: teacher who discovered me at Nuyorican Poets Café, 1992; D. Nurkse: teacher who nurtured me; Estha Weiner: teacher who has matured me since 2006 and my classmates: Sarah, Alan, Julie, Kryssa, etc.; Hudson Pier Poets, especially Stephanie Dickinson and Chocolate Waters; Miriam Stanley; Joshua Meander; Evie Ivy; Chris Robin; Kat Georges; Peter Carlaftes; J. Lois Diamond; Jessica Feder-Birnbaum; Viviana Duncan; Maria Neuda; Marty Davey; Jim Fitzpatrick; Linda Schwartz; Lydia Sklar; Craig Tobias; James Bryant/SpoFest; Rick Christiansen/SpoFest; Jonie McIntire/Uncloistered; Patty Gross; Alby Gates; Chuck Hier; Dr. Guervaz/Ayurveda; German Jaramillo of Eneslow; Pilates: Yaasmin; the dear departed: Barbara Liss, Harry Ellison, Arlene Wege, Larry Mallory, Maxine and Stan Willner, Rabbi Harold Swiss, and Carol Schoen

Contents

Storm   71

Hurricane

Dissipation

Disturbance

Apostle

Bless me Mother for you are gone;
I still sin in the hallowed halls of cinema.
Nay, I am wiped clean after each showing.
Like an apostle, I followed you, mother,
followed you, queen of the double feature,
followed you into forgetting myself,
you, hard edges.

You taught me to bless the moving image—
sweet and tart fruits doled out
in two-hour portions. You taught
me to slip into other skins as easily
as we slipped into disappearing.

There was no need for the talk between us—
the cinema sirens showed me their game.
Natalie, Doris, Elizabeth, Marilyn: Bad girls
and good, seduced by rock-hard jaws.

When the show was over,
I returned to wanting
what you could not reach,
returned to waiting,
waiting to live,
to sin, to be cleansed
in the hallowed cinema
of beginnings, middles, ends.

When the show was over,
we'd walk the two miles home,
pink slowly fading from your flushed face,
puffy mouth and eyes receding into rigid lines,
your love for cinema tucked back inside
that place I could never find.

Supper Time

Mother never cooked like grandmother did,
her mother, Katie, with ingredients
from scratch, took an hour to prepare,
a whole morning to get done,
filling the apartment with warmth.

My mother reduced food
to its driest, flattest state; broiled
what should have been babied
on top of the stove,
or tenderly minded inside.

My mother would throw under the broiler
flesh or fish, never look until edges curled
into the same brown, no matter what
it started out, until it toughened up
like a wrestler punching my teeth and gums
as I tried to chew. No sauce on top,
no salt, no spices.

I couldn't talk much for all the effort needed
to eat the halibut or dry white chicken.
I couldn't complain, couldn't ask for things
I wasn't getting, like allowance or summer camp,
couldn't plead with her to stop hitting me, stop
screaming; all I could do was chew and chew,
get through supper time.

Colors

In the yard, popular girls in fifth
grade surround me, laugh at my green
blouse and blue skirt, "Your colors
clash, your colors clash!" My head
is bowed so low, I can only see pink
poodle skirts above black and white
saddle shoes. The bell rings, taunts stop.

Inside again, Miss McGovern begins
the art lesson. We repeat after her,
"Primary colors are blue, yellow, and red."

"Secondary colors are a combination
of primaries: Blue and yellow
make green, red and yellow
make orange, blue and red
make purple. Brown is a mixture
of all colors."

Outside, green grass risen
from brown earth, salutes
sun and blue sky.

At the Gorilla Forest, Bronx, NY

Three times I wave my right hand
at the female gorilla, standing
before me separated by a few
inches of impenetrable glass.

Each time I wave,
she waits, as if deciding
were I friend or foe,
then picks up her left hand,
palm open, folds it closed,
brown eyes searching mine,
as if she were someone's grandmother
come here from the Old Country,
couldn't speak the language,
reaching out to her grandchild.

My name and that odd little word *OK*
were all my grandmother could say in English.
All along our walks to the live poultry market,
neighbors interrupted us—
I never knew if she were the mayor
or the gossip of our Bensonhurst block.
They hugged my grandmother's lumpy body;
she filled their palms with slices
of her famous blueberry cheese Danish,
saving some for me.

She would brush her leathery face
across my cheek, kiss me on the forehead
for being good, whisper *sheine maidele*.
I didn't understand, but the look in her eyes
was sweet as her pastry.

The female gorilla stands before me,
gray hair on her hips, one arm
wrapped tight around two young ones,
the other hand returning my final wave.
I feel her warm brown eyes pulling at me
as I walk away leaving her
pressed to glass.

The Gardener

I knew my Grandma,
her plump, spotted fingers,
cajoling dough flat,
sprinkling a cow's worth of farmer cheese
into each *blintze*.

I knew her naked
on weekend mornings.
I would tie and re-tie corset strings
until the breasts no longer
hung like worries
as I bound them to her.

I knew my Grandma,
but not her eyes:
sunken, tending
to a garden behind them.
I knew her,
but not the colors
of the flowers,
or the land
the garden grew in.

Batter

The last time I saw Grandma's
dark eyes, they were empty
bowls.

When I was a girl, I imagined
her flying across ocean
from a land where everyone was rooted
like trunks cut in half. Better
to have thought of her
springing from bowls of batter
than from between thighs squatting
above a dirt road.

I imagined her arriving here
with perfect English. But,
when I asked, "Where'd you
come from? How'd you
get here?" she said, "OK."
When I complained about math—
she went "ptoo, ptoo, ptoo,"
told her about the monster
in the closet—she smiled.

It was enough to hug Grandma's
box of a body, tower over her
when I was seven, wrap my arms
almost twice around her as I pressed
my cheek to hers.

Together, we worked the *challah* dough—
my long, pale arms—her dark, small ones—
intertwined like braids.

Sometimes, I snatched a still-baking
bread from the oven, devouring
the center.

Chosen Seats

His nose curved like a pot belly stove;
Grandpa was a six-foot-two episode
in my land of five-footers. We'd quietly
walk along Bay Parkway, stopping when
I pointed at *Jujubes* or *Superman* comic books.
When he caught my finger in the foam half
of his evening's *Rheingold* beer,
he poured me my own in a jelly glass.
It's good, it's medicine, he said.

Grandpa rode his wooden rocking chair
in front of the bedroom window like an Orthodox Jewish
cowboy. Traditional leather straps wrapped around his
arms fluttered as if fringes on a suede jacket.

When I read out loud from library books,
he'd point to letters.
On the next visit to the candy store,
we bought a black and white notebook,
mottled like a cow's hide.
He practiced ABCs in capitals and lowercase;
I could not break his habit of writing from right to left.

Once he took me by the hand
down the Parkway to his synagogue,
up a staircase to the balcony,
filled only with women and girls.
Grandpa let go my hand and reappeared downstairs
among hundreds of men wearing caps like his,
swaying, praying, buzzing like bees.
He wet his fingertips to turn the page.
I leaned over the balcony screaming, *Grandpa,*
don't leave me up here, I'm not like them —
I'm your English teacher, I'm your Rheingold girl.

The Apple Merchant

said it was her first time
eating an apple, but had to hide
the truth, having been a seller
in the market two towns over.

She'd bite into each of her wares,
offer only the sweetest.
The buyers found it odd,
then realized it made
their next bite easier.

The devil happened along one day,
noticed Eve's Pink-Lady cheeks,
her Rome-Beauty breasts and ripening
Delicious buttocks. He knew she knew
her way around.

The devil pointed to his choice.
When she bent over
to make change,
he snatched her, planted
her in the Garden.

Adam never really saw
the fruit, only Eve's
extended hand
and her green eyes
holding the seeds.

Stauch's Baths, Coney Island

Grandma rubs Mercurochrome
and mineral oil on my pale,
sand-grit skin. I round
my back, hide
hint of breast, shine
like orange jellied-candy
dipped in rock-crystal sugar.

I fill my pail, shovel out sand shapes.
Bubbe unwraps our lunch:
onion and herring, seeded rye.

Later, we return to Stauch's lockers.
I unzip her skirt-suit— her arms
can no longer reach back.

She joins friends baking on the roof.
This time, I watch Grandma
behind the tall-slat wall.
She removes the towel: Puckered
flesh naked, breasts swing
browned and full. I turn away,
not knowing how to get back.

Practice

Good girl, every day did your homework:
Practiced kissing the back of your hand,
leaving perfect lipstick traces.

One starry night, teenage-you fumbles
for the key. Your date looms,
puts his hands gently on your shoulders.
You close your eyes, part your lips.
As his tongue dances with yours,
lipstick smears all over your chin.

Babel

> Yiddish was developed from Old High German in the 9th-c.
>
> —*The Cambridge Encyclopedia, 2nd Edition*

"Macht schnell," my boyfriend says
in his best German General tone,
nudges me to hurry, make our train.
Not *that* 'macht schnell,'
not *those* trains.
More like my grandfather calling me
to steaming matzoh ball soup, his thick
glasses fogged, yarmulke askew.

Soup of misshapen dumplings, rough-hewn carrots.
Brothers accusing brothers, born from the same broth.
"Needs a pinch of this"
or "too much of that."
Bless those who do not live
starched to the white page.

Guardians of the Good

I had a hundred unhappy men
under me, who never had a woman
boss, certainly not a slight girl.

Openers, Verifiers, Packers handled
incoming mail for U.S. Customs.
When I spoke, they cat-whistled
and wiggled their middle fingers at me.

After the Floor Captain grabbed
a cache of videotapes off
conveyor belts, men jammed
into the projection room, examined
them for anything beyond missionary.

I heard their braying, kept to my office,
cataloging pornography by violation and country
of origin: Denmark, Sweden, Holland.

When the Floor Captain burst
through my door, licking
his lips, he slapped
the day's haul of magazines on the desk,
took bets on my stammer and blush.

After a while, I slept
with one eye open
while America rested easy.

A Kid and a Dog

you often see that in pictures.

Growing up, I only knew
black dogs in Brooklyn, traveling
in packs, thrashing
at my pant legs, drooling
pus and foam.

As a teen, I had no choice,
but co-exist with a Doberman
who humped my leg on the sofa
while my fiancé moved to second base.
My future in-laws howled with laughter
when their pet walked on the kitchen table
between plates piled with brisket.

Years later, I dashed down a busy thoroughfare,
came upon a German Shepherd,
dazed and bleeding. For an hour,
I frantically flagged unyielding traffic.
When my tears fell on him, I wished
he'd rise up, transform, find his flock.

He raised his head, looked deep
into my eyes. I cradled him
like I never could the fetus
ordered from my womb by a husband
too young to marry.

Feels Quite Natural

these days to walk, immobile
fingers eagled, clutching
our mobile devices, thick
thumbs pressed on the artery
of send/receive.

We forget the grace
of arms gliding through air,
forget the trusting animal
trying to lick our palms.

Heads down, we text and search—
can tell you how many
Samaritans are left.
We can train
our pets to beg,
cannot manufacture
hope in their eyes.

American in Cuba

At the *Museo Bellas Artes Habana*,
preschoolers tell me their families
bring them here often. Everywhere,
girls and women, like strutting
bouquets, in hand-sewn cotton dresses;
boys and men, heads under hoods
of '50s American cars—
breathing deep the smells of Miami.

I stroll near the hotel, arm myself
with *No me moleste* and
Policía, ayúdeme, por favor.
A dark-skinned, young man approaches,
speaks little English; I understand him to say:

"Need your help, don't want your money,
give you my *pesos* for dollars.
Good things only
in dollar stores. Please,
pretty lady." He shows me
his ration coupons—hardly enough—
begs me to help him. I am considering

his request, when *la policía* swoop out,
slam him into a wall, ask for his papers,
my passport, and whether he's bothering me.
"No problema," I say, but they drag him off.
He calls out, "I just wanted to talk to you."

Buzz

From his lifeguard chair,
he watches her emerge
from the ocean, golden skin
bedecked with seaweed.

It stings she won't say back
I love you.

The buzzing in his head becomes
bees swooping, leave him
quaking in the chair.

If he could nail those bees
to the sky, test
each one's intentions,
he'd regain the throne.

His thoughts fly dizzy:
All he wants are her *forevers*,
no more *just nows*.

Approaching, she leans in
to kiss him, whispers something
he can't discern over
the unceasing buzzing.

I Was Kept from Matches

My wedding day started
in pajamas with pink lambs,
night ended in peekaboo
black lace.

After work, after cleaning,
cooking, dishes, my husband
was waiting for me
to assume the position.

First match I lit
started seven years
of hand-rolled joints, shared
with strange, eager mouths.

Offspring

Mother was a sand dune;
I was a camel.

On each birthday, she'd whisper:
"I wish you were
never born." Other days,
she'd throw her body across mine
to block incoming sneeze.

If she'd been vanilla pudding
or Lucille Ball, I might've become
a mother. Gave up on babies
for the first bad boy
and rock 'n' roll was born.

Today's your birthday, my Philodendron.
You've done well 'though I water you
only when I notice your head bowed.

Early on, I almost lost you
when you pushed against
the small pot. Now,
lean and lanky at ten,
you still produce new leaves.

I still taste sand.

Bouquet

Oh yes, I was ready,
all set to slide him under my bed—
still close, but oh so out of reach.

I had folded him up
after he started to show up
beer drunk, barking at me
to spread and lift, his voice stiff
between loose lips, his penis
straightening right to business,
his weight flattening my heart.

Yes, I was ready to press him between
Dan the Mountain Man and the Professor,
who signed his notes to me "Fondly,"
graduating to "Love Forever,"
rolling back down to "Best Regards."

Yes, I'm ready, but I open the door to him
behind a bouquet of roses, some frozen
in cut bud, a few proud in bloom,
others undecided.

Foreigners

Paris! After five years of dreams,
we arrive. Framed by miles of trees,
we stroll the Champs-Élysées, through scenes
rendered in paint and ink for centuries.

I point out to you a door surrounded
by layers of scalloped molding:
"…like an onion," I say.
"A door is just a door," you say.

In a sidewalk café, you enjoy *laissez-faire*
in *Ralph Lauren* khakis, blow
cigar smoke in my face through lunch.
I am green as a Parisian garbage-
worker's jumpsuit.

Standing on a corner, we propose
opposite routes.
Conjuring up my guide-
book French, I ask locals
pour le best direction au the Eiffel Tower?

You step away, look at me
as if I were a mime
suddenly turned standup.

We join the line to the Tower, wait
an hour to reach the first level,
another two to the top.

After we take in all four views,
you give me a kiss: Structured
and pointy as the juncture
we've reached.

Old Pictures

My grandmother would have carried
grandfather if her back
were better.
She did everything else
for him.

After her death,
the police kept hauling him
lost and bewildered back to our house.
He crawled out again and again
to look for her.

My mother-in-law tended
to her starched husband.
She died still praying
he would go first.

But for nosey neighbors,
he would've starved facing
food-filled cupboards.

I sit in front of two laden
plates on the kitchen table.
My husband is very late—
his key turns in the door.
He's pleased I haven't eaten.

Ode to an Acorn

I took you from his gravesite
on the day of the unveiling:
You: hard on the outside;
Father: barely wrinkled.

Perhaps you were in his knickers
when he escaped on a steamer
bound for Ellis Island,
rattled around
when he stopped short,
fell out of his suit pocket
when they lifted the casket.

Little acorn,
on you is writ,
"Here lies a life
not fully lived."

You are planted
on my shelf
next to books
of my poetry
Father never got
to open.

From Nothing

Thank you, Father, for six months of silence
after I broke curfew. I begged and begged you
by paper airplane and alphabet soup
to talk to me.

When you finally spoke, it was
breakfast choices, math equations.

There *were* whispers of your long-ago
escape in a hay wagon, the hasty
voyage to Ellis Island for an eight-
to-a-bed-life on Hester Street.
I wanted to hear more,

but you didn't talk about the forced
rifle-curfews, breaking of glass
in Proskurov, a sister's legs gang-
smashed: History on which to hang
the six-sided yellow star
you gave me for graduation.

I inherited your flat feet. Thank you,
Father: They led me
to fields of rustling quills
and emptied sky
on which to write.

Low Pressure

Queen of the Late Bloomers

She lies casketed in bed
trembling with demands.
The nurses approach with cereal:
Every day she asks for cream of wheat,
then insists she didn't.
The daughters arrive—
her barks spin them away.

As a girl, she'd sought attention
at the piano. Yet, through time,
she exiled us all, except
for a pale man in a black suit,
now waiting at the end of the bed.
He looks at her as if she were his ingénue—
on his feet patent leather shoes,
his hand extended decidedly toward her.

She brushes a dry wisp from her forehead.
Giddy as a girl on the high end of a seesaw
she summons her daughters, allows
the powdering, rouging.

Her breath comes rapidly. The man in black floats
closer to take her hand. The daughters recall years
mother would forbid dancing. Now, she waltzes
onto the patio past the late blooms.

Queen

I am Queen of the world.
Here, the bed covers know
my turning them down;
the tufted rug surrounding this bed
like a moat
has forgotten the imprint
of the King's toes—
trod upon solely by its Queen's
gold-slippered feet.

I rule over everything green
in my three-room palace,
including the cut, bagged, and frozen.
I am holder of the red flyswatter
bequeathed me.
I am holder of circumstance—
granting a week's stay
in my kitchen to a winged one,
allowing to persist
butterflies in my stomach.

"Plain Jane"

they called her.
"I don't need any of you,"
she'd say.

Today, she belongs
to a choir. Sunday morning,
her white robe glistens. Underneath,
Jesus soothes the fresh welts,
darkly rainbowed.

He forgiveth her sin
of plainness, her sins
of Saturday night.

Pierced, collared, bound—
she awaits, center stage.
Whips ascend, descend:

Her breasts sway
from sting after sting,
her back and arms receive the offerings,
thighs accept the love, melt
with every stroke.

"Forgive me, Jesus," she intones.
"On Sunday, I'm yours.
On Saturdays, *I'm*
the anointed."

At the Butterfly Conservatory
After Frida Kahlo's Diego on My Mind

Legs no longer matter—
I have wings! Flutter
from host to host, then choose
a particular girl. Skimming
her multi-hued tattoos, I land
on top of her ebony hair
like a black and orange comb.

Her all-in-leather man
looks astonished
as if a Spanish lady
had replaced his pierced,
studded girl. He swats
at me, pulls at her arm,
but we are steadfast.

When ready, I lift off,
warning her, "Always stop
to look in the mirror," then
spread my wings like a pair
of black eyebrows joined
beneath a third eye.

On Stravinsky's "Rites of Spring"

My hips sway forward
float back
butterflies flutter through
notes snake my feet
bound me to earth
my neck bobs, arms buoy,
sounds sip at my loins—
I unfurl in petalled clarions.

Lot's Wife

So many times, Lot said
Eyes straight ahead.
My peripheral vision
caught him with maidens
by the roadside,
and I said nothing.

How many times
he'd walk ahead, order me
Follow, carry the pots,
grain, keep your head down,
while we lost our way.
When I would say *Let us beseech*
assistance, he'd turn around,
his steel stare withering
my muscles to jelly.

One day, God said *Leave,*
said if we looked back,
we'd be turned into pillars
of salt. I looked back, didn't care
what Lot was up to.
For one sweet second,
I was the pillar.

Glancing Back

Before the last conversation,
I'd stare at your sun-drenched face
on the ride back
from Rhode Island weekends,
the cleft in your chin reminiscent
of the famous Douglas family,
laugh lines decorating eye corners
like bookends, brows furrowed
like fields we'd pass.

After the last conversation,
you exited my front door,
glanced back,
mouth a goodbye slit,
face become marble –
lines stretched tight like sheets
finished with hospital corners
I never could get right,
no matter how many times
you showed me.

Earthworms and Dragons

Hundreds of earthworms
we called bloodsuckers,
when I was a girl,
appeared out of nowhere
when it rained.

Boys chased us, wiggled them
one at a time in our faces.
We shrieked and hid.
If those scary things came
close, they'd become dragons,
sprout wings, breathe fire and smoke,
carry us away.

When I was a girl, my mother's
varicose veins bulged
like earthworms trapped
under skin. Over the years,
my right calf swelled, forgot
its dancer's shape.

As I lay face down, strapped
to the table, the knifeless surgeon
injected a laser into the dead vein,
pulled out the instrument slowly.

As the Doctor warned,
thick white smoke
poured from my mouth
while the vein burned inside me.

I flapped my arms.
Dragon Girl!

Inchworm

It folds in section upon section,
pushing off by slow degree
across the kitchen countertop.
I stop chopping, place
a slice of carrot on the path.
Softly changing course, it's steadfast
in silken, yellow-white skin.

"That's not an inchworm,
but a maggot," I'm told.
Instantly, it glows cold green,
leaves slime in its wake.
Hundreds follow, ooze
out of cabinets, fell
even the strongest among us.

Unaware of my thoughts,
its solitary crawl continues.

Dessert

Her mouth slides slowly along
the proffered spoon—chocolate
ice cream lighting her eyes.
A minute ago, they were blank
when he asked, "Do you know
who I am, Mom? I'm your son."

If she could still talk
to these people circling
the hospital bed, now center-
stage in her living room,
she'd remind them
her favorite is vanilla.

In the Face of
For Uncle Jim

We are waiting for a good man
to die—his sentence
not swift enough.

He won't answer
the phone, let us tell him
his deep voice
had sung us
into family.

At last, an audience is granted.
He's thin as the rake he dragged
through fields as a boy.

Heavy-lidded, he cannot
look at us; heavy-tongued,
he cannot speak.

A good man has died—
his body no longer
lit by radiation.

Dirt covers his casket until
the final sliver of oak disappears.

Tonight, the silent moon
wears his face.

Blessed Work

> All Angels' Church in Manhattan developed
> The Sleeping Bag Project for the homeless.

It's come my turn at the soup kitchen
to make me a sleepin' bag.
Good thing my aunt taught me the 3Rs
and sewin' and cookin' too, 'though
these days I'm rootless, Lord,
like one of them thrown away
Christmas trees cut off at the knees,
blowin' from corner to park.

Sure's a long needle the 'min'strator lady's
handin' me, already's got thread.
There's cloth scraps on the long table.
The lady's sewin' at one end;
I plunge the needle in at the other end.
It springs outta my hand, starts puttin' down
a long straight stitch with a top loop,
like the letter "p." What's that for—
poor? Sure, I begs a little,
I'm no thief, no tramp.

The 'min'strator's tellin' us,
"Keep the stitches clean, the rows
even—be diligent." Guess that means
finish before the snow come.
I try again—feels good to go deep into layers
like the needle's sproutin' roots.

Wherever I lays me down to sleep,
I'll be bound to the ground.

The lady's stitches comin' to meet mine.
How large I want the sleepin' bag opening?
Better try it out: I lift one foot—wings
graze my face! "Go away! I can still
hear the wind, still feel some o' my toes."

Holiday in Pamplona

> Annual running of the bulls has taken
> place in Spain since Medieval times.
>
> —Randy James, "A Brief History of the
> Running of the Bulls"

Heat rides with me in the back
of the truck. I pray
to stay steady on the stones,
slippery with blood and fear,
run safely ahead of horns and hooves,
be alive at the end.

Every other day, I am rooted to the ground
like the 900-year-old olive trees I tend.
I pick up fallen fruit, collect them
in the canvas sack around my neck.
Every night, I sleep shrouded in sweat,
dream of silent trees surrounding me,
stuffing my body into a bag.
When the sun rises, they let me out.

We arrive in Pamplona. I start off
slowly, bulls a good distance away.
I blink—they are at my back,
then, screams, a pileup of runners,
beating of hoof on bone.
I run like a saint on fire—
the cursed canvas bag drops from my neck.
My lungs escape from their slatted cage.

I dart like a swallow
through the *plaza de toros*,
burst into the ring, fall to my knees,
the bulls right behind me. I bless
San Fermin. For three minutes,
I am faster than any bull. Pride
sticks to me like morning dew.

One by one, the animals enter the ring.
They each stand, wounds trickling,
before the unmoving matador.
They will die this afternoon;
I will return to the silent groves.

Road to Feast of San Estevan

> Acoma Reservation contains one of the oldest
> continuously inhabited cities in the United States.
> —J.M. Weatherford, *Indian givers: how the Indians*
> *of the Americas transformed the world*

The tour bus is four hundred feet up
on a sandstone mesa—Acoma Pueblo,
behind a rim of rocks. The guide introduces us
to tribe members standing alongside pottery—
traditional and new designs.

I imagine a Great Creator in the Sky
giving the inhabitants short stature
and square hips to withstand sweeping winds.
Unlike me, with narrow waist and spider legs.

Feast of San Estevan fills the square.
Families cooking reminds me of strudel-making
with my Brooklyn *bubbe*. Except for olive skin,
we didn't appear related. I tell our guide,
"You look very much like my Grandmother—
plucked from Eastern Europe, re-planted across ocean."
Stepping over a tree's exposed roots, she replies,
"Remember, the road goes both ways."

Storm

Holiday on Crete

I sit on a beach chair behind Hotel Nestor
on Rethimno's shore, far
from my Brooklyn-Jewish beginnings.

Three blondes grab sunny spots, remove
their tops, summon the waiter, Costas.
Giggles greet his advancing profile, slipped
from a Greek coin. *Willkommen auf Kreta*,
he says and takes their orders in German.

I remember Costas' stories: Uncle Leonidas
hiding in caves from Nazi invaders; the wail
of his aunts, Elena and Irini, hands locked,
dancing off fortressed walls into the Old Venetian
Harbour; thousands of glider troops descending
around them, blackening the Cretan blue, blue sky.

Costas asks the girls if they've been to the Palace
of Knossos, famed for the Minotaur, half-man,
half-beast. "You won't get lost—signs are in Greek
and German." "Oh, Costas, we are Frankfurt
schoolteachers on vacation. *Das genugt.*
You and the beach are all we need on Crete."

As I head off to join my guide, Costas passes,
muttering under his breath. He lays out
the dinner settings, wipes each knife clean.

Demokratía

> Four Colonels seized power over Greece
> in 1967 and were overthrown in 1974.
> —C. Kassimeris, "Causes of the 1967 Greek Coup"

"Dirty hippies," spat the Athens police,
clubbing sleeping-bagged feet. Long hairs
were dragged from the American Express line
as they waited in Constitution Square.

The aroma of *retsina* and fear hung
n the blue sky. Theodorakis was banned
from the radio. We sat in crowded cafés,
tried to appear calm when locals said,
"Once taken, never returned. Waiters
and taxi drivers may be informants."

We Americans asked how this happened
in democracy's birthplace. The response:
"U.S. fleet in our harbor for years—
not cruise-ships. Our Colonels must say
evkaristó each time they accept your dollars."

At night, young Greek men escorted us
to clubs. We bought stacks of white
dinner plates, *Opa!,* smashed them against
mosaic floors, *Opa!* Each crescendo covered
the web of whispers.

My Eyes Are Tantalized

by Colombian fruits with names like *lulo*
and the taste of acrid tears.
My ears are seared by tales of Black September:
Thousands of slashed bodies bent
the boughs—beggars, prostitutes, orphans.

Traveling up the Andes, I keep my head down,
knock on the tin door of a family *indigena.*
I've come to show them how to count,
how to write their names.

Their last teacher was struck down, sipping
a cup of *yerba buena,* while preaching
it's not the sole purpose of the living
to aspire to heaven, but first,
to conspire to live in peace.

Kingdom

She was too beautiful under the lacy
crown of bride. Dark curls and eyes
had drawn me to claim her.

How had it come to this?
Beauty still present, but unyielding.
Her heart once pounded against my chest
as I opened her until it rained rosewater.

Now, a vessel has ruptured—
I've almost died.
She has stopped bleeding—
a fearful crone guards her entrance.

I've lost my wife, gained a mother,
dictating how much, how fast, how often,
stopping me in mid-bite.

I can only retreat to my porcelain kingdom,
lock the door, take the throne.
I spread open my *Fanny Hill*, imagine
her bottom under my hand.

Here, I never worry about my job,
never stammer and blush.
It's a simple kingdom: Pressure rises,
it's released—my sad heart knowing
it too will burst one day.

Namesake

Father always listens to Mother.
In dreams, he plays poker, goes
bowling, feels the "Attaboy, Harry!"
slaps on his back.

Finally, a bowling-league nephew kidnaps
him. Shoes on, giddy, he steps up to the line—
an old, first-timer. He throws the ball low.
It does a slow-mo down the gutter.

Face reddening, he throws
the second ball high: Strike!
He crumples onto the alley: Stroke!
Lies there, pulse fading
inside his living dream.

Mourning over, I finally get
my first pet: a hermit crab.
For a year, I watch him run
across the rug, tell him stories
of his namesake, Harry.

Starting vacation, I leave a large shell
next to his small one plus plenty of water
and carrots. I return to an empty
exoskeleton, next to his desiccated, little,
pink body lying in front of the entrance
to his big, new home.

Ruse of the Flute

On the afternoon ride to my Uncle's,
I can't stop giggling at Mother's jab
that his hairpiece looks like a slab
of chopped liver. "Stop laughing
like a hyena," she says.

After the trip home, I practice flute
to Mahler's No. 9. The first sweet notes
calm me, until pounding almost unhinges
the door: Five-foot-one-Mother curses me
in Yiddish-English, eyes spinning, teeth
bared in a two-fisted drive to send me
back to unborn.

Her face the same as earlier, on our afternoon visit,
when she passed the den, caught me
on my Uncle's lap. She didn't catch
my attempts to move away, or
his increasing pressure on my wrist,
or the vise around my waist, skewering me
onto the terror underneath, growing.

Behind the Door

I hear the whisk whisk down the hall—
warn you of the impending broom.
We're both spider-legged creatures:
I, with two long ones; you, with four
on each side. I cling to my bed,

you rule your corner of the room,
shrewdly spinning your web
behind my door—always kept
half-open—Mother's orders.

We bond over her intrusions.
Me: Curled around my pillow;
You: Eight eyes of encouragement
to spill my daily dread:

"The pipsqueaks in 6th grade kicked me
again today. What should I do?"
You twirl gracefully around
a single strand. Long legs are good!

I worry about mother looming outside.
Here she comes with the broom!
You scoop up your therapist's shingle,
eight-leg-it out of here.

Thefts

Our kisses began in elevators, then marked
park benches under Coney Island fireworks.

Tonight, we climb the rungs
of the lifeguard chair. He had waited
until night misplaced moon.

I tuck my handbag under the seat,
open my mouth to a web of kisses.
His hand is a snail
on its way to my shoulder.
Fingers slip under my scoop neck blouse
toward my breast a bit with every breath.
He ensnares my nipple—
I cannot exhale.

He offers a hand to help me down.
I do not take it—
reach for my handbag—
flap's ajar, wallet gone.
We see a figure running across the beach.

He turns away from me.
If he had looked into my eyes,
he would've seen a thief creeping
up the chair as soundlessly
as I had watched my breast
take his touch.

A Jew in Texas

Bereft of stars, the New York girl heads for open country,
ready to be called "darlin'" by every stranger,
never to imagine at her new job a star
could be coming toward her, pinned
to the chest of a "real-live" Sheriff.
"Howdy," he drawls, with a dip of his hat.

While the Law puts his guns on the table,
the Manager whispers, "Girl, see how special you are,"
not telling her every new chicken gets plucked
by the Sheriff and, next week, by his Deputy.
No chance to ask Sally Ann's advice—
one of the other night-shift masseuses—
home again with her croupy kid.

As soon as he's undressed, he says,
"Watch your step, girlie,
keep me happy;
we don't like *your* kind here."
He spreads out like a map.
She starts softly on his shoulders,
fingers shaking,
until he growls, "Harder."

She digs into his flesh,
travels down the Jersey coast of his arm,
through Pennsylvania onto Kansas,
then down Oklahoma to the flat, pink butt
of Texas, with its balls hanging over
into Mexico.

"I ain't happy yet," he grunts,
flips over, forces her hand
like a noose 'round his squat cock.
"Uhn." He's done.
"I'll see *you* next week," he says.
 Eyes screwed tight, she shoves
open the door and bolts.

"You'll be back," the Manager says, unaware
the girl has another job to go to.
In her bag, a pair of kitten heels
underneath the Wall Street Journal.

Short Story

I walk into my neighborhood bar, my place for dates from the personals. I spot him right off since he, blessedly, looks like his photo: Olive complexion, wavy black hair. He says, "Hi, it's me, Steve," then gets up from the stool. "Didn't you say you were 6 foot," I say, "I'm 5' 7-1/2" and you come up to my chest!" "I *am* 6 foot; you're wearing heels." "No, I'm in flats." "Then, you're not the height you say you are," he says. "Look," I say, "I don't want to argue, I've been this tall since thirteen." "Bull!" he says. "Sorry, this is not going to work," I tell him and leave.

He runs behind me, shouting, "You're just like all the other bitch-liars." For blocks, he hurls variations on the theme. Passing the Chelsea Hotel, my long stride finally escapes his short fuse. Ghost of Nancy Spungen looks down at me, Sid behind her.

Express Train Seventies

Jump on   jump in
no measures no weights

jump on   jump off
inhaling man after man
joint after joint

pick-up trucks spinning by thumbs
jump on jump in
sleeping on...
Whose floor is this anyway?

When I Skipped My Hair-Colorist Appointment

The young guy leaning against a pole
on the N train looks like an old boyfriend.
My face forgets its sag and pulls up
a flirty smile. Disrobing the stranger
with my stare, I can still feel my long-ago
Adonis' hair sweeping across my breasts;
his fingers, tongue slowly advancing
beyond once-tightly patrolled borders.

Train lurch shatters my open-mouthed
reverie. The only thing pointing at me now
is the young understudy's engorged disdain:
"Well, look at this, everyone," he says,
"I've got a gray-haired groupie."
I have to laugh.

Illumination

Empty unlit street,
deep cough behind her,
quick, quick, slow, slow –
he follows a Queens beat,
drawing even closer.

She pictures one swarthy arm
bandoliered across her chest,
the other rifling through her.

Her heart beats like a racehorse
overtaking the lamplit intersection.
He's crossed to the other side,
escaping the frame
she's put him into.

The Poet

He said he'd read from the best
in his collection, "My pulsing
prick, her twat, my hot rod –
I fucked that cunt, that bitch's
fucking cunt."

He read another and another
and the cunts piled higher
as he flung each one
at the audience until he got
his poetical rocks off!

My ex-husband sure missed
his calling: He said those
very same words to me.
At the time, I didn't know
it was poetry.

Hurricane

Mother Said

After Hal Sirowitz

"You're not leaving this house
without your sweater," mother said.
"If you don't take it,
you'll catch cold, it'll turn
to flu, you'll die, then,
I'll kill you!"

Role Model

Thank you, Father, for the *Daily News*
comics, for *Nancy Drew*, for books
you'd hide in the bathroom clothes hamper.

You never knew I'd found them. Age 10,
I had a Master in Literary Porn: *Lolita*,
Fanny Hill, *Lady Chatterley's Lover*,
Story of O.

Yet, the most dog-eared of your secret
treasure was the lone sea-faring tale
of a young First Mate: After years
of all stripe of cruelty, he spiked
the whiskey, then fled the Captain's bed
for the final time.

Oh, Father, we too wanted to escape,
but you never left her. And, you never
stopped her coming at me— week upon week—
nails, fist, rod. "You know your Mother,"
was all you'd say.

Mother, I knew your wrath, but not
your biggest secret: My sweet Grandma,
my rock, had made hell of *your* childhood.

Trouble

My ankle bracelet says we are going steady.
We wait until your dad leaves
with his band for the Catskills,
throw on his Stan Getz and Astrid Gilberto's
Girl from Ipanema;
It's Trouble's favorite too,
howling with the buzzing sax sections.

We check at the door
for your mom's raucous snores
before removing our underwear,
spread a towel on the red sofa of crushed velour,
avoiding the broken springs;
kiss until air and song are gone.

We change to Coltrane.
You are sitting on the backs of my thighs
rubbing your penis between them.
Trouble starts humping furiously on my foot.
I move sharply—feel your stab—
a gasp of blood on the white towel;
I throw up; Trouble chews my shoe.

It's one A.M. when you get me home;
my father won't open the door.
I sit bleeding in the cement stairwell
and I can't tell dad I've been broken.

Crak, Bam

After he lifts my veil,
the territory given me
is orgasms like M-16s,
bowling, crushed-
pretzel meatloaf.

On Mahjong night, between
one *Crak*, two *Bam*,
talk of who has the biggest
bedroom set, best vacations,
best chance to get pregnant,

I can't say
I've been sneaking around
with my hippie sister,
eating rice that isn't white,
riding my Brooklyn train
to Washington Square
anti-war protests.

I can't say
I stopped looking *up* to him
after he keeps his eyes closed
during Ella Fitzgerald
at the *Rainbow Room*,
tells me he can't
get past her skin.

I can't say
I stopped looking *at* him
after he marches me
to the Clinic, tells me to say,
"We're not ready."

I am ready to toss
my veil, scorch earth.

Footsteps barely
on new ground—
I fall off the edge.

Naming a Hurricane

When the first cloud shadows
my spooning heart, you cast laughter
over it. I hide the cloud
behind our portrait.

Manna beads from heaven.
When our fireworks interrupt
les bons temps rouler, the lake thrashes
the levees. I try to shore them up;
you argue away the cracks
until I crumble.

Cloud bursts overtake our home
on Harmony Street. You thunder
at life's dropping one shoe; I grab
hands passing. Mudslide takes me
shoeless away.

Disappearances

Cowboy man in navy striped suit,
eyeglasses and pointy-toed boots offers
me a ride, then whips my head around,
hammers my mouth into his lap...

I float out of body above the white Chevy
watch him slide the knife across my throat.
After he's done, I'm pulled back to myself—
dumped onto the road; red neck
above his suit collar fades
from view as his car jumps ahead.

I swivel on stage to "Lady Marmalade,"
see only the pole my red heels clank against,
flashes of sheer black bikini underwear.
I can't make out the audience below.

I hear their breaths hasten, the rough
moving of palms beneath tabletops.
I miss the last step off the platform;
they clap anyway; I forget my name.

You kiss me—I close my eyes.
Heads rotate faster, faster.
Blue light spirals from faces,
lines crease like tributaries.
I open my eyes—you can't read
my mind, you can't read my mind.

Hitching in Dallas

The female half of a bouffant and crew cut,
country-club-couple
rolls down the flag-decaled, passenger window.
Five minutes past her "Get in,"
she moves to the driver's seat,
he hops in the back, next to me,
covers my mouth,
thumbs a ride
up my mini skirt.
He does not hear me say,

"I'm your roadside Jew-girl, fresh
from Coney Island's fun house.
Marvel at my horns, if you dare,
but when you come up behind me,
watch out, I'll swat
your beastly face
with my tail."

All in a Row

He drapes a girdle
around a chair before
his date arrives, rubs against it,
explodes.

He likes the girl,
imagines her form
as armature
for a second skin.

"Nice dress. What do you wear
underneath?"
He looks past

her slender frame, dreams women
in lines, a latex
gauntlet. He pushes through,
naked.

She dreams family lore: A singed sign—
Triangle Shirtwaist Factory,
door bolted, scream
of corseted women at rows
of sewing machines,
a distant cousin, burning.

Brooklyn Rush Hour

My mini-dress rides
halfway to crease of thighs,
triple degrees inside F train.
Droplets down track legs
stuck to man in front
and guy in back
like cheese sandwich
pressed on grill.
Train pounds into stoppings,
starts pull out pounding.
Back guy falling wedges knees,
hint of hand on my backside.
Brooklyn slips by windows,
hand slips past borders.
Guy works hand up dress,
organ pressed to legs—
I am silent red like cut
tomato on shelf.

Seed of scream opens, "Hey,
creep, keep your hands
off me." "Lady," he says,
"I wouldn't touch you
with a ten-foot pole."
"Well sir, I happen to know
you sure don't have
any ten-foot pole."

The Last Word

The gravedigger picks up
a mud-clumped shovel,
pushes it into one of the mounds
insulating my father from worries
that cut short his life.

His younger sister, my Aunt Bethel,
pushes to the front. Guilt
for my father's sacrifices throws her
into the grave on top of the casket.
"Take *me* instead, take *me*," she cries.

The gravedigger isn't sure
whether to lift her out
or throw in dirt. The older sister, Selma,
falls to her knees, beats her chest,
screams, "No, *me*, I've nothing:
Broken engagement, retired from millinery."

My aunts wail, expect my father to rise,
plead with them like always, "Remember
how lucky you are to live in America."

The gravedigger picks up his tools and leaves,
the weight on top of the casket
heavier than any dirt.

Art

I congratulate an acquaintance
at a SoHo gallery on his sale
of a Basquiat. Father interrupts me,
whispers from his grave,
"How could you, Daughter—
don't you remember?"

I remember how he'd come home
scribbled down to a nub, railing
against paint-spray vandals,
"How can they call that art
kids've thrown all over
the city trains!"

Forty years it took him to get
from scrubbing train terminals
to department boss. Then,
the bigwigs demoted him:

Couldn't find the perfect paint-
remover for train-and-trestle-
explosions of color.

Mocked by every kid with a can,
too tired to stop Mother's tirades:
First, he suffered a stroke; last,
a heart attack.

As the monitor pulsed
to a stop, his hospital room filled
with the light of firecrackers
he'd set free as a boy
on Hester Street.

The Tailor

When Grandpa opened the small wooden drawers
under the *Singer*, buttons and thread tumbled
like starving refugees out of hay wagons,
after the "all clear."

His thin feet wore down the paint on the pedal.
He struggled to keep up
with the neighbor ladies' purchases,
his perfect handiwork hidden
under the final pressing.

Months late, they'd badger him
to let out the same garments at no charge,
point out this and that with fleshy arms jiggling,
numbers pressed onto their skin,
stretched wide like in funhouse mirrors.

He never asked for more *gelt*,
never looked in their eyes,
his back stooped
under their demands.

The ladies insisted they hadn't gained weight,
quickly looked away from the mirror
before the beautiful dresses turned
into striped sacks, hanging
like the skin of starving dogs.

The Crow

> Hitler committed suicide
> in a bunker on April 30, 1945.
> —*Encyclopedia Britannica*

We followed his shrapnel tracks
across Western Europe.
If only we could track back, his acts
might be undone; back to when he spoke
through an artist's palette, not yet
with blood-soaked tongue.

When he looked into the pool
of Narcissus, stony eyes glowering,
did he enchant the flocks around him
to see an Aryan god?

Too easy, he may have thought;
more challenging to turn
skin to lampshade,
bone to ash.
"Natur ist grausam," he said.
Nature is cruel.

Oh, Murder's captain,
scavenger of remains!
When the crow goes into a deep
hole and he is finally done,
may veiled eyes see.

Tibet, Land of the Snows

Bound by bamboo to mist mountain,
panda haunch-sits hungry
in the tree den:
a distraught Buddha.

Lumbers about for food,
spies two blank eyes.
Rocks shift, reveal
a monk's body.

Panda slumps safe
against shrub.
Padded feet hook
a bamboo shoot,

growing through a hole
in the monk's riddled chest.
Eating bamboo, eating bamboo—
end-to-blood-soaked-end.

Sister

Imagine being that nun in Guatemala,
the one who got burnt with cigarettes
one hundred-eleven times.
Can your eyes trace the path
of a cigarette spelling in blisters
on your skin the word *puta?*
Do you hold your breath
or gasp it into the pain?

Your torturers turn minutes
of foreplay into days—
thrust church candles into you.
Puta en una capucha (whore in a habit*),*
they spit, batter you with their flesh.
You feel their organs grow to the size
of the wooden cross on which they nailed Jesus.
Is He testing you as you testify
to your love of Him?

Imagine they now hang you above
a local woman who's been bound—the one
who helped you in church reading class.
They force into your fists a machete,
press their hands down on yours to slice
the weapon across the woman's chest—
you've cut off her breasts.
You are shaking, the cut is ragged.

Or would you rather be
one of the rapists? Or their director?
Or the other woman?
Or Jesus? Or His Father?
Choose.

How Do You See Inside a Vortex

Whole world's hooked in place
on the news: whites and blacks,
blacks and blues.

Can't order nevermore for black lives
un-mattered; can't order pandemic
to be demoted to night terror.
Only nevermore we can reach is no longer
swallow our whole tongue (just the tip,
when necessary).

How do you see inside the crack of a wind-
pipe replayed around the world? My recurring nightmare
of black Boston Professor I didn't marry: Police
a threesome on our daily walks, our hand-holding;
their flashlights dimming our longing. I let
those backward winds push me away
from our path, looted.

How do you go from not breathing to breathing?
Inhale your breath, exhale; inhale their breaths,
exhale: Didgeridoo circling the globe blows
the knee off the earth's neck, smashes it to ground.
With only one leg to stand on, ignorance
topples. And we rise on our black-brown-yellow-
white-red feet, toenails starred and striped.

Dissipation

In the Company of Spiders

For *Charlotte's Web* by E. B. White

At least once a week, Mother's face
looks like she's killing Cossacks.
I give up arms folded over my head.
Slapping and scratching, she exhausts
herself, then hugs me. I go limp,
she calls me 'Cold Fish.'

I can't talk to classmates, neighbors,
cousins. I don't care, I have plenty
of friends. My favorite is Charlotte,
waiting for me under the bed.

One night, I open my book to lonely
Wilbur, the pig, meeting Charlotte, the spider.
When he hears he'll be Christmas dinner,
he cries out, "I don't want to die."
Suddenly, neither do I.

Charlotte and offspring weave "Brave",
"Strong" and "Loved" into their webs
for Wilbur and for me.

In the company of spiders, poems
are woven from my diaries, friendships
from paper dolls. Mother's hands turn
arthritic; I finally stop them in mid-air.

Today, tomorrow, I'll swing my spider
legs across the land, Charlotte
by my side, weaving, weaving.

Soft Hand

Mother calls for me in skipping tones;
her legs do not support rising.
She sits shrinking on a bedroom chair,
can't bear the touch of help.

I encircle her thin, spotted hand—
the softness startles—
I do not remember softness.

       Her flying nails had raked skin raw,
       she wielded wire hangers,
       I hid under tables.
       She caught me by the hair
       pulling it along half a house length.

Now her eggshell hand tugs at my skirt.
She cannot poke her bird head
through the sweater neck.
Rivulets of wrinkles run down her breasts,
the nipples bite her belly—
my hard heart shatters.

Morning, Mother

I dress my heart with a black-cut ribbon,
lift the latch on my gate, begin the walk
around the block marking one month
I took a pinecone from your graveside.

I tell you now that in my room
I'd recount on my knees the day's hurts,
pray that you'd suffer that many times.
I'd take it back after breakfast,
Morning, Mother, did you sleep fine?

They carried you out in a pine box— stop
the hearse—the butterflies in my stomach
have lost their wings! I put pennies
into the casket for the time you dragged yourself
four miles to Pitkin Avenue, paid
the pushcart vendor two cents you owed.

The journey back to my gate
is now complete, the ribbon removed.
You are sitting on the edge of a pin
wearing the two pairs of socks
I put into the box to warm
your bloodless feet.

Rock Chick Sonata

I listened to the Top 40 muted under the pillow,
so mother wouldn't yell, kept a list of each song
and artist, put an asterisk when Murray the K announced,
"Moving up to #1, Janis Joplin, "Piece of My Heart."

When mother's tirades ended with my arms
scratched bloody, I squeezed the wounds,
dipped in a pinky, smeared on the bedroom wall
the words "Rock 'n' Roll."

Prayers turned to frenzied leather and runaway
hair. I washed them away before the door
was thrown open, the smell of *Wheatena* wafting in.

After breakfast, mother scrubbed
the floor where the piano once stood,
sold for marriage, along with her
gold medals for Tchaikovsky, etched
with the year mother was fourteen.

When I finally towered over her,
I played air guitar at my wedding.

Now, when mother visits
in dreams, she cries me
a broken record, "Don't you see
why I scratched my sonatas on your skin?
You were my Carnegie Hall."

After Death

Another October passes.
Again, no visit to mother's grave.
Next year.

In life, she was a shoreline hit
by disaster after disaster,
denuded of past,
of future.

I couldn't look beyond her eyes,
couldn't read her.
She was all kisses, all fists.

Fear was the boulder in the doorway,
fear was my surrogate mother.
Yet, I wept at her funeral,
wept on the road emptied of mother.

When we'd walk the same path,
I'd twist myself almost to snapping
to avoid her footprints,
make my own.

Now, I understand her nicotined fingers,
coffee and sugar blasts and blues.
I understand her porcelain dark-haired beauty,
cracked to helpless crone—
no potions to soften her.

I'd refuse my mother's hand
when we walked. Now,
I welcome her into me
to fill in my shoreline,
make me whole.

At Ellis Island

Father leaves his Sephardic
last name in the hay wagon
he escaped in. Blends with
the Eastern European Jews
at Ellis Island.

He settles family in a Brooklyn project.
When father smells one whiff
of cumin-laced lamb, he closes
windows, piles on his plate
brisket and boiled potato.

When he comes upon neighbors, he brushes
past their *Komo estash*, mutters
under his breath, "I'm fine, I'm fine."

When his daughter asks where
he was born, he points far
across ocean. She collects photos
of faces like his: long and narrow, high-
cheekbones, sharp chin, dark eyes.

In school, she slips easily into *Me llamo.*
Señoritas in red beckon
from grammar books. When she decides
to teach Spanish, father yells,
"You're throwing away your education."

Now, he's lost the way
to temple, can't find the next
prayer page.

Every day, she shows him photos
of faces like his. He's forgotten
who she is, forgotten his name.
Every day, he prays,
"Dío, por favor,
take me
to mi padre."

Finding Barbara

My first call to your new room,
semi-private: "It's Madeline."
"I had a friend, Madeline."
"It's me!" "No—it's not."

They moved you from your Manhattan
Apartment to slow your descent, already past
the bunny hill, careening down
the intermediate slope.

I exist outside your assisted oatmeal
and camaraderie. Can you still
recite Frost, sing "Danny Boy?"

These days, to understand one word of yours
is like rescuing a shell-fragment
from a storm-blown beach. After our calls,
I want to give up, but you and I
don't know when we fail or succeed.

As I lose you, I want to curl into a ball, roll
to a corner by the TV. New friends and old
push me onto the up escalator.

In my Queens apartment, I tape dozens
of your travel-postcards together
to keep them from slipping
under the bookcase into the dust.

Divining

Y-shaped
branch, lead me
to my final resting place.

Do not fold my long
thigh bones, boxed. Unplot
the family tree.

Scatter my ash
around maple, stir
wind, tremble leaves.

Branch, musty
as I'll be. Mold, turn
auburn curls green.

Bark, peel off the shaft.
Rod, pull me one way
or another.

Cousins

For decades, your nervous system
is on overload. Today, you call 911:
chest pains. ER doctor sends you home—
a panic attack.

For days on end, your legs are riddled
with pains, as if they're trying to escape
your center, hard-wired for hyper-vigilance.
You sleep in fits.

Our whale cousins rest one side of their brains
at a time. Eons ago, they learned it's better
to be half-relaxed than forever
on high alert or asleep, floating
in danger.

Let your body, overwrought by day,
by night, listen to the whales' songs.
Let them swallow you whole. They sense
they were like you.

Keep a penknife in your pocket. Cut
yourself out each morning. It's OK—
family makes sacrifices.

Now, swim alongside
the whales, take a breath
and breach.

Path of Mary Magdalene

After the *Gospel of Mary*
"discovered in 1896 in upper Egypt."
—*The Gnosis Archive*

I opened my heart
to the Lord, allowed Jesus
to cast out demons, write
on my cave the words,
"You are saved," and I was.

My womb is a vessel
that holds His teachings.
Yet, men like Peter hiss
that the folds of skin between
my legs must harbor sin,
that a woman's body holds secrets.
I was given tongue and lips
with which to spread the truth.

Men like Paul proclaim pain
most holy, mortifying their skin
until it melts. If blessed
is their scourged blood, blessed
is my blood poured forth each month,
blessed is the dying and resurrection
I host each month.

I say unto you, let the Lord flow
through each of us like tributaries
joined at the same source. One path
to Him is through tingling
of nipples, twitching of feet.

Allow Him to rock divine hips.
More truths appear—breath comes faster.
Receive the Lord in liquid moan
and yell, "Oh Jesus, Oh God,
we are come to Heaven."

Candleman

sells Jasmin-scented
possibility.

I take home a triangular candle,
strike a match. Flame stirs
blue-edged like a peacock feather,
wick glows white,
black ash spreads up
from the middle.

I pass my hand above the flame,
reminded that cool colors emit heat,
blow gently engaging fire in dance.

I am cool flesh with waiting wick;
I will wait no more! Take a breath,
heat moves up my spine.

A second breath melts colors.
My core is lit, my spine is a wick.
I do not wait for Candleman.
I do not need a match.

Untethered

There once was a woman
whose long, coltish legs
stopped traffic when she was young,
who gathered hosannas
for her firm, round calves.

She forced her feet into high heels,
pointed in front like the apex
of her beauty. While her legs
enjoyed adulation, the bones
in her feet slowly moved, froze
into the shape of the pointed shoes
she possessed in five different
colors. After a while, every step
she took hardened her smile, drove
pain across nerve.

She vowed to not allow
the rest of her body to freeze.
She stretched her shoulders,
pumped iron.

She remembers the day it happened.
She was rotating her arms, then felt
a bit of lift. She ripped off her heels,
exposing claws, peeled off layers
of designer clothes, folded
her feet under her rump, flapped
a few times and flew off.

Women teetering on spikes
looked up, marveled at the great
eagle flying above them.

Control

My *Jewfro* is freestyling to the funk.
 "Hey, Curly Hair, you dance like a *Sista*,"
says my black boyfriend, doing
the Dance-of-the-Nerd.

WASP guys tell me, "You Jewish girls
are so smart, so wild."
Not *all* of us.

Teenage-me once straightened my hair
with lye. Everywhere, sleek ponytails
and pageboys taunted me. But,
my hair was a lie and the glop
burned me to hell.

Passing through West Virginia, the waitress
hurries me past the few white customers,
sits me in the Kinky-Hair section,
alongside the lone Black.

At the office, my stick-straight-
woman boss often barks, "Control
your hair."

I wake up with it so knotted,
I have to cut it free.

Mango Mad on the Island of Grenada

I cut into slick-hard skin:
A shiny bat flies out
over unlit roads behind slight hotels.
Beating wings spread thick perfume
from split, fallen fruit
until there's no air spared.

I bite into memories of liquid
youth's gushing of soul and body
like movies of vampires' unabashed
blood-drenching in bibbed white shirts.

Sucking nectar from stringy flesh,
I disarm mango rivers like a sweaty
tree-climbing-kid whirling
under an unexpected waterfall.

Since I Was a Young Girl

These days, pool's my thing.
When up, I run the list:
Right leg forward, left leg
back (unlocks my hip),
tilt chin (hides the sag), suck in
belly, slowly bend.
Oh no, I scratch!

When up again, I chalk the stick.
Gentle tap on the cue's sweet
spot makes the long
shot. High fives from my graying
crew as I do the tight-jean-strut,
perfected at *Max's Kansas City*
when I was young.

The Blind Man and Poet

He'd never seen a woman.
Sight is one color in *her* palette.
The way she says his name
sounds like seersucker,
terry cloth, old blues.

They question what is green,
verde, vert.
"It's cucumber," she says.
"Envy's green," he says.

He removes her fine silk blouse.
She closes her eyes.
When he slides fingers down
her silky arm, each inch
announces itself. He traces
the rest of her outline, hangs it
on his mind.

Their breathing's bumpy now.
They empty, smell
like cucumbers, like
new beginnings.

Imagine Your Finger as Scalpel

What do you see in the mirror: Merely shapes or every blemish and flaw? How you look to definers? What would you do if your finger were a scalpel? Growing up, I held *Archie's* Betty and Veronica next to the mirror: They were Venus; I was Pluto. I'd stare at my face throughout the day, redesigning dreamt-of incisions, especially to my nose. Bullies, bullies everywhere: In the family, in the street, in school, screaming at me, "Ugly, ugly." Thicket of bangs met black cat's-eye glasses, above my frozen un-smile. When I stuck a toe in the dating pool, boys had me at the first caress of my face. "So beautiful," they'd say. Never believed it: Knew they used those words to score. Nowadays, my High School and college photos surprise me. I hereby affirm I'm beautiful inside and out. I hereby affirm I'm ugly inside and out. I've put down my finger. Now, please, put down yours.

Rhinestones and Memories

I gave you away to *Reminiscence*, my favorite
store in SoHo, long out-of-business. Now, I see you
in a new second-hand shop, half-hidden
under a pile of other rhinestone purses.
"Hello, old friend."

Remember how we'd bounce from kiss to caress
at Studio 54? I'd wear those bright purple,
elephant bell hip huggers. They always did the trick:
By 4 AM, you'd be stuffed with numbers.

I still wear bright colors. I see your once-
flaming-fuchsia suede has worn
to barely pink. Both of us are scored
with lines but hold spirit enough.

I take you in my arms, unclasp you.
Oh, strumpet! Inside, your glory's
unfaded and ripe! Unfolded,
I too still flush, awakening
the rose.

About the Author

Madeline Artenberg was a street theatre performer and photojournalist before falling for poetry. After her first poem popped out at an open mic, she was encouraged by a teacher in the audience, Denise Duhamel, to take her class at Writers Voice. Madeline sold her camera equipment before the second class. Her work appears in numerous print and online publications, such as *Rattle* and *MacQueen's Quinterly*. She is also a well-known performance poet in NYC.

During 30 years of writing and performing her poetry, she has studied with D. Nurkse; Denise Duhamel, Estha Weiner, Alice Notley; Robert Bly, and many others. In April 2006, *Rogue Scholars Press* published *Awakened*, with poems by Madeline Artenberg and Iris N. Schwartz. *The Old In-and-Out*, a play directed by Kat Georges, based on poems by Madeline Artenberg and Karen Hildebrand, had a sold-out run in NYC in 2013. She co-produced *The Alternative New Year's Day Poetry and Spoken Word Extravaganza* in New York City for 20 years.

Additional accolades include *Mudfish* poetry prize: Finalist (2020); *Best of the Net* contest: poem nominated by *Poets Wear Prada (2020)*; Highland Park Poetry Challenge: Honorable Mention (2017); *Margie, The American Journal of Poetry* contest: Semi-Finalist (2005); Poetry Forum contest: 1st prize (2003), 3rd prize (2013); Lyric Recovery Poetry contest: First prize (1999), Second prize (2000), Semi-Finalist (2000).

Made in the USA
Middletown, DE
26 May 2023